Easter Activities

imagine THAT!™

Imagine That! is an imprint of Top That! Publishing plc,
Tide Mill Way, Woodbridge, Suffolk, IP12 IAP, UK
www.topthatpublishing.com

Contents

Recipes

Recipes continued

Activities

Getting Started

Making your own food and creating your own crafts is great fun and really quite easy. Best of all, everyone will enjoy what you create!

Measuring:

Use scales to weigh exactly how much of each ingredient you need, use a measuring jug to measure liquids, or use a ruler to measure craft materials.

Mixing:

Use a spoon, balloon whisk or electric hand whisk to mix the ingredients together.

Different ideas:

Decorate your cakes and biscuits with flavoured or coloured icing, and then add chocolate drops, sweets or sugar strands. Experiment with different colours and craft materials.

Different shapes:

Cookie cutters come in lots of different shapes and sizes, and can be bought from most supermarkets. If you don't have any cookie cutters of your own, carefully use a knife to cut out the shapes you want.

Creativity:

Once you've made a recipe or craft in this book a few times, think about whether you could make your own version. Why not mix some chocolate chips into the Banana Custard or try drawing a rose instead of a sunflower? This way you can start to make up your own recipes and activities. Try to think up names for the things you create!

Read through each recipe or activity to make sure you've got all the ingredients or equipment that you need before you start.

Always ask an adult for help if you are not sure about anything.

Cooking Equipment

Before you begin to get creative in the kitchen, it's a good idea to take a look through the drawers and cupboards to make sure you know where all the cooking equipment is kept.

• To complete the recipes in this book, you will need to use a selection of everyday cooking equipment and utensils, such as mixing bowls, saucepans, a sieve, knives, spoons and forks and a chopping board.

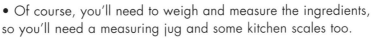

• Of course, you'll need to weigh and measure the ingredients, so you'll need a measuring jug and some kitchen scales too.

• Some of the recipes tell you to use a whisk. Ask an adult to help you use an electric whisk, or you can use a balloon whisk yourself – you'll just have to work extra hard!

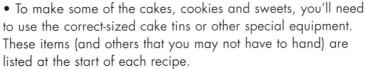

• To make some of the cakes, cookies and sweets, you'll need to use the correct-sized cake tins or other special equipment. These items (and others that you may not have to hand) are listed at the start of each recipe.

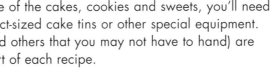

• Please note: The temperatures and measurements given in this book are approximate. Use the same measurement conversions throughout your recipe (ounces or grams) to maintain the correct ratios.

Craft Equipment

The activities section in this book is packed full of fun things to make and do!

• Before you begin the arts and crafts in the activities section, you will need to gather together a variety of materials, such as scissors, glue, felt, card and paint. All of this, plus anything else you need can be found in all good craft or hobby shops.

• Some of the activities can be very messy! If this is the case, make sure you cover your work surface with an old cloth or newspaper, wear old clothes and remember to wash your hands after handling equipment such as glue or paint.

• Always ask an adult to help you when using a needle, scissors or any other sharp object.

• The most important thing to remember is to have fun, and be patient!

  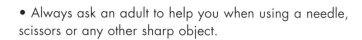 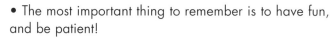  

Safety and Hygiene

It is important to take care when cooking and doing craft activities as there are lots of potential hazards and hygiene risks.

- **Take Note! Whenever you see the warning triangle you will need adult supervision.**

- Before starting any cooking always wash your hands.

- Cover any cuts with a plaster.

- Wear an apron to protect your clothes when cooking or using craft equipment that could stain.

- Always make sure that all the equipment you use is clean.

- If you need to use a sharp knife to cut up something hard, ask an adult to help you. Always use a chopping board.

- Remember that trays in the oven and pans on the cooker can get very hot. **Always ask an adult to turn on the oven and to get things in and out of the oven for you.**

- Always ask an adult for help if you are using anything electrical or sharp – like an electric whisk, scissors or needles.

- Be careful when heating anything in a pan on top of the cooker. Keep the handle turned to one side to avoid accidentally knocking the pan.

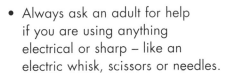

- For craft activities, always make sure your work surface is covered with newspaper and wear old clothes.

- Keep your pets out of the kitchen while cooking.

Recipes

Hot Cross Buns

It wouldn't be Easter time without hot cross buns – this home-made recipe is great to make all year round!

Hot Cross Buns

1 Sift the flour, salt and spices into a large bowl and mix in the yeast, raisins, rind and sugar.

2 Next, add the butter to a saucepan, stir in the milk and vanilla extract and ask an adult to heat until warm. Whisk in the egg, then add the warmed mixture to the flour mixture. Form a dough by kneading the mixture on a floured surface for 10 minutes until it is smooth and elastic.

3 Divide the dough into 12 buns, cover with a damp tea towel and leave in a warm place for about 90 minutes, until doubled in size.

4 Mix all of the paste ingredients together and put it into an icing syringe. Pipe a cross on each bun and bake in the preheated oven for 10 minutes. Reduce the heat to 150°C and bake for a further 15 minutes. Meanwhile, mix together the glaze ingredients and lightly brush the buns, before leaving to cool on a wire rack.

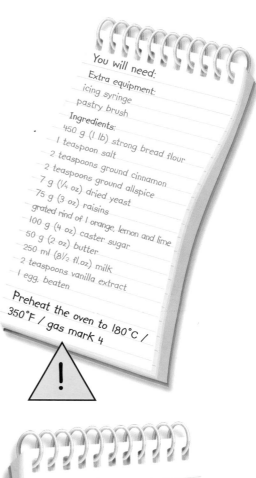

You will need:
Extra equipment:
icing syringe
pastry brush
Ingredients:
450 g (1 lb) strong bread flour
1 teaspoon salt
2 teaspoons ground cinnamon
2 teaspoons ground allspice
7 g (¼ oz) dried yeast
75 g (3 oz) raisins
grated rind of 1 orange, lemon and lime
100 g (4 oz) caster sugar
50 g (2 oz) butter
250 ml (8½ fl.oz) milk
2 teaspoons vanilla extract
1 egg, beaten

Preheat the oven to 180°C / 350°F / gas mark 4

For the paste:
75 g (3 oz) plain flour
2 tablespoons sugar
100 ml (3 fl.oz) water
For the glaze:
2 tablespoons brown sugar
3 tablespoons milk
1 tablespoon marmalade

Chocolate Eggs

These yummy chocolate eggs will melt in your mouth!

Chocolate Eggs

1 Dampen a piece of kitchen towel with a little sunflower oil, and polish the inside of each mould.

2 Next, break the chocolate into small, even pieces and ask an adult to melt gently in a bowl over a saucepan of hot water, making sure the bowl is not touching the water. Place a cooking thermometer into the chocolate and heat until it reaches 43°C / 110°F. Take off the heat and cool to 35°C / 95°F.

You will need:
Extra equipment:
cooking thermometer
greaseproof paper
8 x small egg moulds
palette knife
foil (optional)

Ingredients:
300 g (10 oz) chocolate
(70% cocoa solids)

Top Tip!
Collect some brightly coloured foil and wrap your home-made eggs - they make great presents!

3 Pour spoonfuls of the chocolate into each mould and swirl around until coated. Leave to set, flat side down and covered in greaseproof paper. Fill each mould the same way. Leave to set for 20 minutes, then repeat the process for another two or three times to build up a good layer of chocolate. Ask an adult to draw a palette knife across the chocolate to ensure a clean edge. This is important so that the two sides of the egg stick together evenly. Leave to chill until set.

4 Carefully unmould the egg halves, taking care not to handle the chocolate too much as it will start to melt. To stick the two edges of an egg together, heat a baking tray and then place the edges of two halves on it for a few seconds, then gently push the edges together. Take care as the tray will be very hot.

Crackle Nests

Use cornflakes or crisped rice to make these little cakes crackle!

Crackle Nests

You will need:

Extra equipment:
paper cake cases

Ingredients:
25 g (1 oz) sugar
25 g (1 oz) butter
2 tablespoons cocoa
1 tablespoon golden syrup or honey
25 g (1 oz) cornflakes

To decorate:
sugar sprinkles
coloured chocolate eggs

1 Put the sugar, butter, cocoa and golden syrup or honey into a pan over a low heat. Stir until the ingredients have melted.

Top Tip!
Use crisped rice instead of cornflakes if you prefer.

2 Stir the cornflakes into the mixture until they are completely coated.

3 Spoon a little of the mixture into each of the paper cases. Top each nest with sprinkles and coloured chocolate eggs, then leave them to set.

Spring Sponge

Make this fab cake for your whole family to enjoy!

Spring Sponge

1 Put a cake tin on a sheet of baking parchment. Draw around it and cut out the shape. Place inside the cake tin and repeat the process for another tin.

You will need:

Extra equipment:
2 x 18 cm (7 in.) cake tins
baking parchment
electric whisk
sieve
spatula

Ingredients:
100 g (4 oz) butter
100 g (4 oz) caster sugar
2 eggs
100 g (4 oz) self-raising flour
50 g (2 oz) strawberry jam
50 g (2 oz) whipped cream
15 g (½ oz) icing sugar, to decorate

Preheat the oven to 180°C / 350°F / gas mark 4

Take Note! Ask an adult to help you use the electric whisk.

2 Ask an adult to mix the butter and sugar together with an electric whisk. Next, add the eggs and continue to whisk.

3 Sift the flour into the mixture with a sieve and fold in using a spoon. The mixture should be light and creamy – if it isn't add a drop of milk.

4 Divide the mixture between the cake tins and gently spread out with a spatula.

5 Ask an adult to place the tins in a preheated oven for 20–25 minutes. Allow to cool, then remove the cakes from the tins.

6 Add the jam and cream to the top of one cake, then sandwich both cakes together. Sift icing sugar on the top of the sponge, then serve!

Gingerbread Chicks

Create your own gingerbread chicks with this great recipe!

Gingerbread Chicks

1 Use a paper towel to grease the baking tray with a little margarine.

2 Sift the flour, bicarbonate of soda, ground ginger and ground cinnamon into a mixing bowl.

3 Put the margarine, pear and apple spread and concentrated apple juice into the saucepan over a low heat, and stir until melted.

4 Ask an adult to pour the melted margarine mixture onto the flour in the bowl. Mix the ingredients to form a firm dough.

You will need:

Extra equipment:
baking tray
rolling pin
cookie cutters
icing syringe

Ingredients:
100 g (4 oz) plain flour
½ teaspoon bicarbonate of soda
½ teaspoon ground ginger
½ teaspoon ground cinnamon
25 g (1 oz) margarine
1 tablespoon pear and apple spread
1 tablespoon concentrated apple juice

Preheat the oven to
160°C / 325°F / gas mark 3

For the icing:
100 g (4 oz) white chocolate
ready-to-roll icing
orange paste food colouring
edible eye decorations

5 Put the dough onto a floured surface and gently roll it out (not too thinly) with a rolling pin. Cut out chick shapes, putting them onto a baking tray as you go. Collect the dough trimmings into a ball and roll them out to make more biscuits. Bake in the oven for 10–15 minutes, then cool on a wire rack.

6 Put the white chocolate into a heatproof bowl. Ask an adult to place the bowl over a pan of simmering water, making sure the bowl is not touching the water. Dunk the bottom of your chicks into the melted chocolate.

7 Put a few drops of orange paste food colouring onto the ready-to-roll icing and roll it out until the colour is evenly spaced. Ask an adult to cut out the different shapes for the chicks' feet and beak using a sharp knife. Stick the pieces on to the gingerbread using melted white chocolate.

8 Stick the edible eye decorations onto the chick biscuits with melted white chocolate to finish.

Egg-ilicious Biscuits

Let your imagination run wild when you decorate
these egg-tastic biscuits!

Egg-ilicious Biscuits

1 Use a paper towel to grease the baking trays with a little butter. Put the butter into a bowl, add the sugar, and mix them together until they're light and fluffy.

2 Add the egg, mixing it in well.

3 Sift the flour into the bowl. Gently mix in the flour, and then use your hands to knead the mixture into a smooth dough. Wrap the dough in cling film and put it in the fridge for 15 minutes.

4 Put the dough onto a floured surface, and sprinkle a little flour onto a rolling pin. Roll out the dough (not too thinly), and cut out egg shapes. Put the biscuits onto a baking tray and bake them for 10 minutes, until they are golden brown. Lift them onto a wire rack to cool.

Top Tip!
Soften the butter by taking it out of the fridge 30 minutes before you need to use it.

5 Use water icing to decorate the biscuits. Sift the icing sugar into a bowl and add enough water to make a smooth paste. Swirl the icing onto the biscuits and decorate with sugar sprinkles to finish.

You will need:
Extra equipment:
2 baking trays
rolling pin
cookie cutters
icing syringe
Ingredients:
100 g (4 oz) butter
100 g (4 oz) caster sugar
1 egg
225 g (8 oz) plain flour

To decorate
100 g (4 oz) icing sugar
1-2 tablespoons hot water
sugar sprinkles

Preheat the oven to
180°C / 350°F / gas mark 3

Raspberry Towers

These pretty layered biscuits will go down well at any party!

Raspberry Towers

To make the shortbread:

1 Place the butter and sugar in a bowl and mix together well.

You will need:
Extra equipment:
sieve, rolling pin,
cookie cutter, baking parchment
electric whisk, icing syringe

Ingredients:
For the shortbread:
100 g (4 oz) butter
75 g (3 oz) caster sugar
160 g (5½ oz) soft flour
15 g (½ oz) ground rice
For the filling:
300 ml (10 fl.oz) whipping cream
300 g (10 oz) fresh raspberries
small spray of fresh mint leaves
15 g (½ oz) icing sugar

Preheat the oven to 200°C / 400°F / gas mark 6

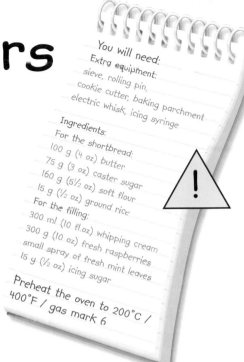

2 Sieve the flour and ground rice into the mixture and stir. Mix to a smooth dough, cover and chill in a refrigerator.

3 When cold and firm, divide into two halves and roll each using a dust of flour until it is 3 mm (¼ in.) thick.

4 Use a cookie cutter and cut out round circles. Prick with a fork to prevent rising.

5 Line a baking tray with baking parchment and cook in a preheated oven until golden brown. Store in an airtight tin when completely cold.

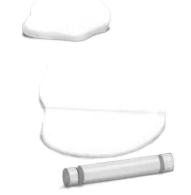

To make the towers:

6 Ask an adult to whip the cream until stiff.

Take Note! Ask an adult to help you use the electric whisk.

7 Using an icing syringe, pipe a ball of cream in the centre of the shortbread.

8 Arrange the raspberries neatly around the cream and press another shortbread on top.

9 Repeat the process and pipe a neat ball of cream on the top and decorate with a single raspberry and a pair of mint leaves.

10 Place on a serving plate and dust with icing sugar to finish.

Cupcake Nests

An irresistible treat for those with a sweet tooth!

Cupcake Nests

Take Note!
Ask an adult to
help you use the
electric whisk.

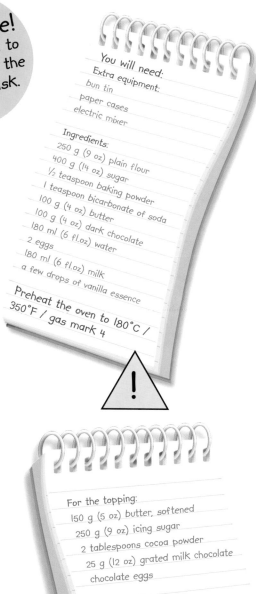

You will need:
Extra equipment:
bun tin
paper cases
electric mixer

Ingredients:
250 g (9 oz) plain flour
400 g (14 oz) sugar
½ teaspoon baking powder
1 teaspoon bicarbonate of soda
100 g (4 oz) butter
100 g (4 oz) dark chocolate
180 ml (6 fl.oz) water
2 eggs
180 ml (6 fl.oz) milk
a few drops of vanilla essence

Preheat the oven to 180°C /
350°F / gas mark 4

⚠️

1 Put the paper cases in the bun tin.

2 Put the flour, sugar, baking powder, bicarbonate of soda and butter in a large bowl. Mix together.

3 Next, ask an adult to melt the chocolate in a heatproof bowl over a pan of hot water. Make sure the water doesn't touch the bottom of the bowl.

For the topping:
150 g (5 oz) butter, softened
250 g (9 oz) icing sugar
2 tablespoons cocoa powder
25 g (12 oz) grated milk chocolate
chocolate eggs

4 Add the water, eggs, milk, vanilla essence and melted chocolate to the flour mixture.

5 Ask an adult to beat the mixture at a low speed for 30 seconds with an electric mixer. Then, beat at a high speed for 3 minutes.

6 Use a teaspoon to transfer equal amounts of the mixture to the paper cases. Bake the cupcakes for 20–25 minutes. Leave them to cool on a rack.

7 For the topping, beat together the butter and icing sugar. Combine the cocoa powder and water, and add to the mixture. Beat until smooth and creamy. Spread over the cupcakes, sprinkle with grated chocolate and top with chocolate eggs.

Banana Custard

Mmm ... this custard is fab on its own or accompanying a dessert!

Banana Custard

You will need:
Equipment:
electric whisk

Ingredients:
300 ml (10 fl.oz) full fat milk
1 vanilla pod, split in
half lengthways
3 large egg yolks
1 tablespoon cornflour
2 tablespoons demerara
sugar
2 bananas, cut into slices
whipped cream, to decorate

1 Pour the milk into a saucepan and add the vanilla pod. Next, ask an adult to bring the milk to a boil over a medium heat. As soon as it boils remove the pan from the heat and scoop out the vanilla pod.

Take Note!
Ask an adult to help you use the electric whisk.

2 Tip the egg yolks into a bowl, along with the cornflour and sugar and whisk until the mixture is thick.

3 Pour the hot milk into the egg mixture, whisking until well combined.

4 Pour the custard mixture back into the pan. Add the sliced banana, reserving a couple of slices for decoration, and heat gently over a low heat, stirring all the time, until the custard thickens. Add a dollop of whipped cream, topped with a sliced banana to finish. Serve hot or cold!

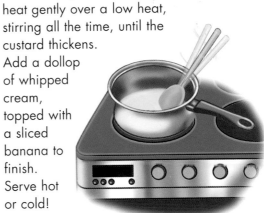

Strawberry Cheesecake

This heavenly cheesecake is easy to make and simply scrumptious!

Strawberry Cheesecake

1 Put a loose-bottomed tin on a sheet of baking parchment. Draw around it and cut out the shape. Grease the tin with a little butter and place the baking parchment inside. Then, put the biscuits in a plastic food bag and crush using a rolling pin.

2 Transfer the crumbs to a bowl, then pour over the melted butter. Mix thoroughly until the crumbs are completely coated.

3 Tip them into the prepared tin and press firmly down into the base to create an even layer. Chill in the fridge for 1 hour to set firmly.

4 Ask an adult to prepare the vanilla pod, by slicing lengthways, then scraping out the seeds using the back of a knife.

5 Next, place the soft cheese, 100 g (4 oz) of icing sugar and vanilla seeds in a bowl, then ask an adult to beat with an electric mixer until smooth. Tip in the cream and continue beating until the mixture is completely combined. Next, spoon the mixture onto the biscuit base. Smooth the top of the cheesecake down with the back of a spatula and leave to set in the fridge overnight.

6 Once the cheesecake has set, remove from the tin and place on a serving plate.

7 Ask an adult to purée the strawberries in a blender with 50 g (1 ½ oz) of icing sugar and 2 teaspoons of water, then sieve. Swirl the purée onto the cake with a knife.

You will need:
Extra equipment:
23 cm (9 in) loose-bottomed tin
baking parchment
plastic food bag
rolling pin
spatula
electric mixer and blender
Ingredients:
250 g (9 oz) digestive biscuits
100 g (4 oz) butter, melted
1 vanilla pod
600 g (1 lb, 3oz) soft cheese
150 g (5½ oz) icing sugar
250 ml (10 fl.oz) double cream
100 g (4 oz) strawberries, hulled and sliced
2 teaspoons water

Take Note!
Ask an adult to help you use the electric whisk and blender.

31

Jewel Jellies

These wobbling jellies will liven up any party!

Jewel Jellies

1 If using fresh fruit, wash and prepare it to start with. Cut the strawberries in half and cut the other pieces of fruit into small slices.

You will need:
Extra equipment:
jelly moulds
heatproof jug

Ingredients:
135 g (5 oz) pack of flavoured jelly
300 ml (10 fl.oz) boiling water
150 g (5½ oz) mixed fresh or frozen berries / fruit

2 Place the jelly into a heatproof measuring jug and ask an adult to pour over 300 ml (10 fl.oz) of boiling water. Stir with a spoon until the jelly has dissolved.

3 Stir the fresh or frozen fruit into the jug.

4 Pour the mixture into six individual jelly moulds or into one big mould. Place into the fridge to set for at least 3 hours.

5 To unmould the jellies so they are ready to serve, ask an adult to half fill a bowl with hot water. Dip the jelly moulds, one at a time, briefly in the water and then lift out and quicky place the serving plate over the top. Flip the plate over and remove the mould. If you are using one big mould, ask an adult to cut the jelly into portions with a knife.

6 Decorate with extra berries for a pretty finish and serve with ice cream!

Butterfly Buns

These butterfly buns are topped with pretty wings!

Butterfly Buns

1 Put the paper bun cases in the bun tray.

2 Put the butter and sugar into a mixing bowl. Use a wooden spoon to beat them together until the mixture is fluffy and very pale in colour.

3 Beat in the eggs, one at a time, adding a tablespoon of flour with each one.

4 Sift the rest of the flour into the bowl. Use a tablespoon to mix the ingredients gently, as if you were drawing a figure-of-eight. This will make sure your mixture stays nice and fluffy.

You will need:
Extra equipment:
a bun tray
paper cases
sieve
Ingredients:
100 g (4 oz) butter
100 g (4 oz) granulated sugar
2 eggs
100 g (4 oz) self-raising flour
glacé cherries, to decorate
For the buttercream icing:
80 g (3 oz) butter
150 g (5½ oz) icing sugar
1–2 tablespoons milk
food colouring (optional)

Preheat the oven to 190°C /
375°F / gas mark 5

5 Use a teaspoon to transfer equal amounts of the mixture to the bun cases. Bake the buns for 20–25 minutes or until they are well risen and golden brown. Leave them to cool on a wire rack.

6 To make the butterfly wings, cut a slice from the top of each cake. Now cut each slice in half.

To make the buttercream icing:

7 Use a wooden spoon or an electric mixer to beat the butter in a large bowl until it is soft.

8 Sift half of the icing sugar into the bowl, and then beat it with the butter until the mixture is smooth. Then, sift the rest of the icing sugar into the bowl and add one tablespoon of milk.

9 Beat the mixture until it is smooth and creamy.
Now, add a couple of drops of food colouring if you want to.

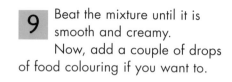

10 If the mixture is too thick, add a little extra milk to make it more runny. Add extra icing sugar if you need to thicken the mixture.

11 Place a little buttercream icing on top of each bun. Now, gently push two of the halved slices into the icing on each bun at an angle to form pretty butterfly wings! Top with half a glacé cherry to finish.

36

Chocolate Truffles

A box of these chocolate truffles makes the perfect present!

Chocolate Truffles

You will need:
Extra equipment:
paper sweet cases
plastic container

Ingredients:
200 g (7 oz) plain chocolate
200 ml (7 fl.oz) double cream
25 g (1 oz) butter

To coat the truffles:
cocoa powder
chocolate strands
desiccated coconut

1 Ask an adult to put a heatproof bowl over a saucepan of just-simmering water. Make sure the bowl doesn't touch the water. Break the chocolate into small pieces and put them into the bowl, and then add the cream and butter. Stir the mixture until the chocolate has melted.

2 Take the saucepan off the heat. Take the bowl off the saucepan and leave it to cool for a few minutes. Carefully pour the melted chocolate into the container. Put the lid on the container and leave it in the fridge to set for 3–4 hours.

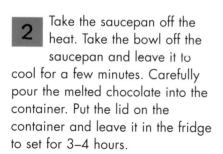

Top Tip!
You'll have to roll the truffle balls quickly or the mixture will literally melt in your hands! Why not roll the truffles in chocolate strands or desiccated coconut?

3 Remove the container from the fridge. Roll small balls of the chocolate mixture in your hands.

4 Roll the balls in cocoa powder, and then put them into the paper cases. Store the truffles in a container in the fridge until you're ready to eat them or give them as a gift.

Coconut Ice

These simple sweets can be made in any colours you like!

Coconut Ice

1 Put a tin on a sheet of greaseproof paper and draw around it. Cut out the square so that it is large enough to overlap the sides. Then, slit the corners and put it inside the tin.

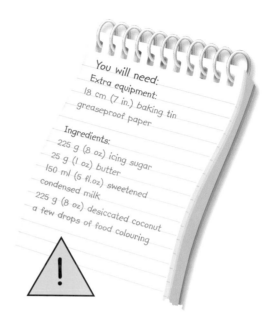

You will need:
Extra equipment:
18 cm (7 in.) baking tin
greaseproof paper

Ingredients:
225 g (8 oz) icing sugar
25 g (1 oz) butter
150 ml (5 fl.oz) sweetened condensed milk
225 g (8 oz) desiccated coconut
a few drops of food colouring

2 Ask an adult to help you put the sugar, butter and sweetened condensed milk into a pan over a medium heat, and bring the mixture to the boil. Let the mixture simmer for 4 minutes, stirring all the time.

3 Remove the pan from the heat and stir in the coconut.

4 Ask an adult to pour half of the mixture into the tin. Leave it to cool.

5 Colour the other half of the mixture with a few drops of food colouring. Pour it on top of the mixture in the tin, and leave it to set. Cut the Coconut Ice into squares, but be careful – it will be very crumbly!

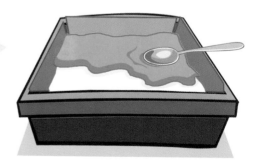

 Daisy Cakes

Use lots of brightly coloured icing to decorate these flowery buns!

Daisy Cakes

1 Put the paper bun cases in the bun case baking tray. Sift the flour into a bowl.

2 Put the flour and margarine in the bowl. Use the tips of your fingers to rub the margarine and flour together until the mixture becomes crumbly.

3 Add the sugar and mix it in. Now stir in the egg. Finally, add enough milk to make the mixture creamy.

4 Put spoonfuls of the mixture into the paper cases. Bake the cakes for 10–15 minutes, until they are golden brown, then leave them to cool on a wire rack.

You will need:
Extra equipment:
paper bun cases, sieve, bun case baking tray, cookie cutter, icing syringe (optional)
Ingredients:
225 g (8 oz) self-raising flour
75 g (3 oz) margarine
75 g (3 oz) caster sugar
1 egg
75–100 ml (3–4 fl.oz) milk
Water icing:
100 g (4 oz) icing sugar
1–2 tablespoons water
food colouring (optional)
To decorate:
ready-to-roll icing
yellow sweets
Preheat the oven to 180°C / 350°F / gas mark 4

Top Tip!
You could decorate your cakes with sugared diamonds, sugar sprinkles, silver balls or small sweets!

Decorating the Cakes

1 Cover the buns with water icing. Here's how to make it! Sift the icing sugar into a bowl. Add 1–2 tablespoons of hot water and mix until you have a smooth thick paste. Add one or two drops of food colouring if you want coloured icing. Fill an icing syringe with the water icing and carefully pipe onto the cakes. Leave to set.

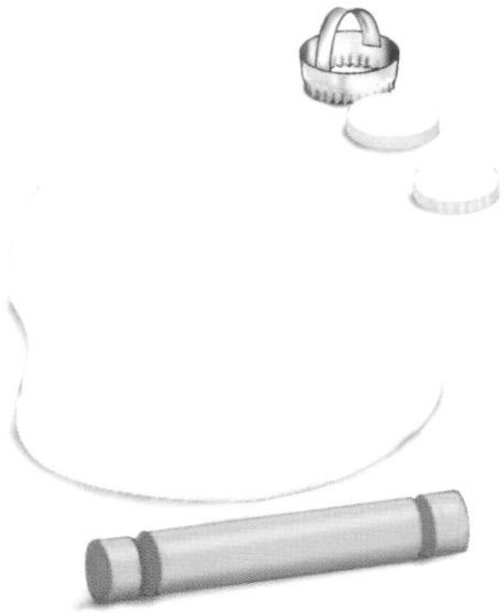

2 Roll out the ready-to-roll icing with a rolling pin. Using a cookie cutter, cut out circle shapes.

3 Next, ask an adult to cut out the different petals using a sharp knife. Run a knife carefully along the top of each petal, before placing them over the set water icing, gently pressing down. Top with a yellow sweet to finish.

Top Tip!

To make chocolate icing, add one teaspoon of cocoa powder to the icing sugar before sifting. To make lemon icing, add 1–2 teaspoons of lemon juice instead of hot water.

Try out these variations for your cakes:

Chocolate Chip Buns

Sift 25 g (1 oz) cocoa into the bowl with the flour. Mix in a handful of chocolate chips. When the buns are cooked and cooled, cover them with chocolate water icing (see method above).

Coconut Buns

Add 50 g (2 oz) desiccated coconut to the mixture with the sugar. When the buns are cooked, top them with lemon water icing (see method above) and sprinkle them with more coconut.

Cherry Buns

Add 100 g (4 oz) chopped glacé cherries to the mixture with the sugar. When the buns are cooked, cover them with lemon water icing (see method above) and top each bun with half a glacé cherry.

43

Fab Fruit Kebabs

Choose your favourite fruits to make colourful fruity kebabs!

Fab Fruit Kebabs

You will need:
Equipment:
skewers

Ingredients:
a selection of fresh fruits:
strawberries
seedless grapes
pieces of kiwi
pieces of orange
pieces of mango
pieces of banana
pieces of pineapple

1 Wash and prepare the fruit to start with. Cut the strawberries in half and cut the mango, orange, pineapple etc. into thick slices.

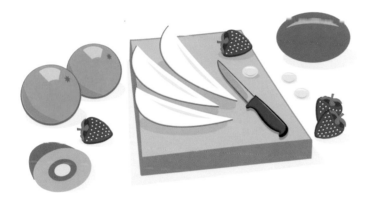

2 Push the fruit onto the skewers, alternating the different types of fruit.

Top Tip!
Try this with lots of different fruits. Which combinations work best together? Drizzle with strawberry sauce from page 31 for a fab finish!

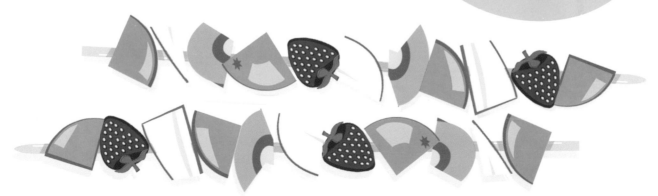

Carrot Cake

This scrummy carrot cake won't stick around for long!

Carrot Cake

1 Put a cake tin on a sheet of greaseproof paper. Draw around it and cut out the shape. Grease the tin with a little margarine and put the greaseproof paper inside.

2 Sift the flour and baking powder into a bowl. Add the sugar, walnuts, raisins and carrots and stir them together well.

3 Add the eggs and oil to the bowl. Beat all of the ingredients together until they are well mixed.

4 Spoon the mixture into the prepared tin, spreading it all, and smooth the top with a spoon. Bake the cake for one hour, or until it is firm to the touch.

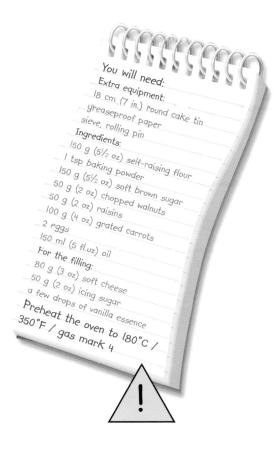

You will need:
Extra equipment:
18 cm (7 in.) round cake tin
greaseproof paper
sieve, rolling pin
Ingredients:
150 g (5½ oz) self-raising flour
1 tsp baking powder
150 g (5½ oz) soft brown sugar
50 g (2 oz) chopped walnuts
50 g (2 oz) raisins
100 g (4 oz) grated carrots
2 eggs
150 ml (5 fl.oz) oil
For the filling:
80 g (3 oz) soft cheese
50 g (2 oz) icing sugar
a few drops of vanilla essence
Preheat the oven to 180°C / 350°F / gas mark 4

To decorate:
water icing (see pages 42-43)
ready-to-roll icing
orange and green paste
food colouring
pistachio nuts, grated (optional)

47

5 Once it has cooled, remove from the tin and ask an adult to cut the cake in half with a sharp knife.

6 To make the filling, mix the icing sugar, cream cheese and vanilla essence together. Spread the mixture over the top of one cake half. Then, carefully sandwich the two together.

7 Make the water icing using the instructions on page 43. Pour the icing all over the cake, spreading it down the sides and over the top.

8 Next, put a few drops of orange paste food colouring onto three-quarters of the ready-to-roll icing and roll until the colour is evenly spaced. Ask an adult to cut out small carrot-shaped pieces with a sharp knife. Stick the pieces around the top of the cake.

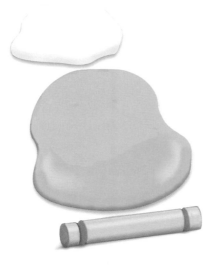

9 Repeat the process with the leftover icing, this time with green paste colouring. Add little balls of icing to the top of the carrots, pressing gently to stick. Finish with a sprinkling of pistachio nuts in the centre of the cake.

Chocolate Brownies

These gooey brownies make a perfect school holiday snack!

Chocolate Brownies

1 Beat the eggs and the sugar together in a bowl, until light and fluffy.

2 Melt the butter and beat in the cocoa powder, before adding to the eggs and sugar. Sift the flour and fold into the main mix with the pecans.

You will need:
Extra equipment:
sieve
20 cm (8 in.) baking tin
greaseproof paper
Ingredients:
2 eggs
225 g (8 oz) caster sugar
100 g (4 oz) butter, melted
3 tablespoons cocoa powder
100 g (4 oz) self-raising flour
50 g (2 oz) pecans, chopped
For the fudge icing:
50 g (2 oz) butter
1 tablespoon milk
100 g (4 oz) icing sugar
2 tablespoons cocoa powder
pecan or walnut halves, to decorate
Preheat the oven to 180°C /
350°F / gas mark 4

3 Put a baking tray on a sheet of greaseproof paper. Draw around it and cut out the shape. Grease the tin with a little margarine and put the greaseproof paper inside. Pour the mixture inside and bake for 40–45 minutes.

To make the fudge icing:

4 Melt the butter and add the milk. Remove from the heat, then beat in the icing sugar and cocoa powder.

5 Spread the icing over the cooked brownie and decorate with pecans or walnut halves. Cut into squares when the topping is firm.

Chocolate Fudge

A wonderful treat for anyone who loves chocolate!

Chocolate Fudge

1 Put a baking tin on a sheet of greaseproof paper. Draw around it and cut out the shape so that it is large enough to overlap the sides. Then, slit the corners and put it inside the tin. Ask an adult to help you put the chocolate and the condensed milk into a saucepan over a medium heat. Add a few drops of vanilla essence and stir them together until the chocolate has melted.

You will need:
Extra equipment:
15 cm (6 in.) baking tin
greaseproof paper

Ingredients:
300 g (10 oz) plain chocolate
200 ml (7 fl.oz) sweetened
condensed milk
a few drops of vanilla essence

Top Tip!
Add white or dark chocolate to make different flavoured fudge!

2 Ask the adult to pour the mixture into the tin, and smooth the top with the back of a spoon. Put the tin into the fridge for 3–4 hours.

3 Remove the fudge from the tin by lifting it with the greaseproof paper. Turn it out onto a board and peel off the paper. Cut the slab of fudge into squares and serve!

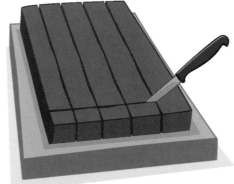

Spring Garden Cupcakes

Inspired by a beautiful garden in bloom!

Spring Garden Cupcakes

1 Put the paper cases in the bun tin.

2 Crack the eggs into a bowl and beat lightly with a fork.

3 Place the butter, sugar, flour and vanilla into a large bowl. Add the beaten egg and a couple of drops of green food colouring.

4 Beat with an electric mixer for 2 minutes, until the mixture is light and creamy.

5 Use a teaspoon to transfer equal amounts of the mixture to the paper cases. Bake the cupcakes for 18–20 minutes. Leave them to cool on a wire rack.

6 For the topping, beat together the butter and icing sugar. Once well mixed, add the vanilla, food colouring and water. Beat until smooth. Swirl over your cupcakes and decorate with flowers. If you use real flowers, remember to remove them before eating!

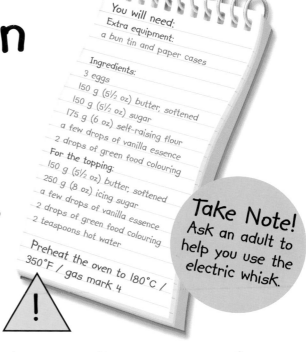

You will need:
Extra equipment:
a bun tin and paper cases

Ingredients:
3 eggs
150 g (5½ oz) butter, softened
150 g (5½ oz) sugar
175 g (6 oz) self-raising flour
a few drops of vanilla essence
2 drops of green food colouring
For the topping:
150 g (5½ oz) butter, softened
250 g (8 oz) icing sugar
a few drops of vanilla essence
2 drops of green food colouring
2 teaspoons hot water

Preheat the oven to 180°C / 350°F / gas mark 4

Take Note!
Ask an adult to help you use the electric whisk.

Chocolate Pots

Eat these heavenly chocolate pots before they melt!

Chocolate Pots

1 Beat together the eggs, egg yolks, sugar and cornflour until well mixed.

You will need:

Extra equipment:
whisk, 6 ramekins,
foil, roasting tray

Ingredients:
2 eggs
2 egg yolks
15 g (½ oz) caster sugar
1 teaspoon cornflour
570 ml (1 pt) milk
100 g (4 oz) dark chocolate
4 tablespoons chocolate and
hazelnut spread
50 ml (2 fl.oz) whipped cream,
to decorate
grated chocolate, to decorate

Preheat the oven to 180°C /
350°F / gas mark 4

Take Note! Ask an adult to help you use the electric whisk.

2 Ask an adult to heat the milk until nearly boiling. Gradually pour the hot milk into the egg mixture whilst whisking.

3 Next, heat the chocolate and chocolate spread in a bowl over warm water.

4 When the chocolate has melted, whisk into the egg mixture.

5 Grease six ramekins with a little butter and pour in the mixture. Cover the tops with foil and place in a roasting tray.

6 Fill the tray with water halfway up the dishes, and place in a preheated oven for 30–40 minutes or until the chocolate has set.

7 Remove from the tray and chill until required. Decorate the tops with whipped cream and a little grated chocolate.

Colourful Cookies

These colourful cookies are so delish, you'll want to make them again and again!

Colourful Cookies

1 Cream the butter and sugar together in a bowl, until light and fluffy. Add the egg and mix well.

2 Sift the flour into the creamed mixture and, using your hands, create a smooth, firm dough. Refrigerate the mixture for 15 minutes.

3 Roll the dough out on a floured surface until it is 5 mm thick. Using either a sharp knife or cutters, cut out various shapes and transfer to a greased baking tray. Bake in the oven for 10 minutes or until golden brown.

4 Cool the cookies on wire racks.

5 To make the icing, sift the icing sugar into a bowl. Add 1–2 tablespoons of hot water and mix until you have a smooth thick paste. Add one or two drops of food colouring if you want to. Spread the icing over the cookies, using a palette knife or spoon to add detail.

6 Next, transfer the icing to an icing syringe and pipe finer details onto the cookies. Decorate with additional sweets if desired.

You will need:
Extra equipment:
sieve
rolling pin
cookie cutters
palette knife
icing syringe

Ingredients:
100 g (4 oz) butter
100 g (4 oz) caster sugar
1 egg
225 g (8 oz) plain flour
assorted sweets

Preheat the oven to 180°C / 350°F / gas mark 4

Top Tip!
Remember, wash the icing syringe thoroughly before changing the colour of the icing!

For the icing:
100 g (4 oz) icing sugar
1–2 tablespoons water
food colouring (optional)

Banana Milkshake

Blended with apricots and frothed with ice cream,
this is the mother of all milkshakes!

Banana Milkshake

1 Place the apricots, banana and jam in a blender and ask an adult to whizz the mixture into a smooth purée.

You will need:
Extra equipment:
blender

Ingredients:
3 handfuls apricots, chopped
(fresh or tinned)
1 large banana, sliced
2 tablespoons apricot jam
4 scoops vanilla ice cream
360 ml (12 fl.oz) milk

Take Note!
Ask an adult to help you use the electric blender.

2 Add two scoops of ice cream. Keep the blender running, gradually adding the milk until frothy. Pour into two glasses.

Top Tip!
Tinned apricots are ideal in this rich and creamy shake.

3 Add another scoop of ice cream to each glass. Top each with a straw and cocktail umbrella and serve!

Mud Pie Shake

Make this chocolate milkshake as muddy as you like with a combination of chocolate flavours!

Mud Pie Shake

1 Place all of the ingredients into a blender and ask an adult to whizz the mixture until smooth.

You will need:

Extra equipment:
blender

Ingredients:
4 scoops chocolate ice cream
375 ml (12 fl.oz) milk
dash chocolate syrup

Take Note!
Ask an adult to help you use the electric blender.

2 Pour into two glasses, top with straws and serve immediately.

Top Tip!
Crumble, or grate, some chocolate on top and create a muddy puddle topping.

Activities

Creative Cards

Make these cool cards for all of your friends and family!

Creative Cards

1 Using a large (3 cm) daisy punch, cut four daisies out from the front corners of the card. Keep the cut-out daisies for later.

2 Glue the pearlescent 12 cm paper on the inside of the card, so the shiny side shows through the daisy shapes at the front.

3 Using the 3 cm punch again, cut four daisies from the second piece of pearlescent paper. Using a 2 cm medium punch, cut out eight daisies from the vellum paper and a 1 cm punch to cut 16 daisies from the white paper.

4 Ask an adult to shape the petals with a pair of scissors to create a more flower-like appearance.

You will need:
3 daisy punches, 3, 2 and 1 cm in diameter
card, folded to 12.5 x 12.5 cm
2 sheets of pearlescent paper,
12 x 12 cm
vellum paper
white paper
ribbon, tied into a bow
glue (paper and silicone)
scissors
pens or pencils

5 Glue the card daisies over the cut-out daisies on your base card, but at a twisted angle, so you can see the pearlescent paper underneath. Glue the four large pearl daisies in-between the card ones.

6 Glue the vellum paper daisies to the top of all the large daisies.

7 Colour the centres of all sixteen small daisies: light yellow first, followed by a half moon of orange yellow, finishing with tiny orange dots in one half of the centre.

8 Glue the small flowers to the top of all the large daisies, then glue the remaining eight flowers in a circular pattern as shown in the main picture.

9 Finish by sticking the ribbon to the front of the card.

65

Egg Hunt

Host an egg hunt for your friends!
You'll have a great time!

Egg Hunt

1 If you are taking part in the hunt yourself, ask an adult to hide the eggs around the chosen space, whether it is a garden, field or house, depending on the weather. Ask them to hide the eggs in clever places, for example, hidden up small trees, in flower beds or long grass.

You will need:
30 small foil-wrapped eggs, or more / less depending on how many people are taking part
baskets or containers
a small prize

3 Award the person who finds the most eggs a small prize. In the event of a tie, ask an adult to hide another egg – the person who finds this one is the winner!

2 Gather your friends together and give each of them a basket in which to collect the eggs. Explain that there are 30 eggs hidden and they need to find them. Count down from 5 and shout 'Go'!

Papier Mâché Letters

Spell out your name with these colourful letters!

Papier Mâché Letters

You will need:
a bowl
wallpaper paste
water
newspaper strips
poster paints and brushes
an old cloth or newspaper

1 Place the wallpaper paste, water, and lots of thin, torn-up strips of newspaper into a bowl.

Top Tip! Cover your work surface with newspaper or an old cloth to avoid making a mess!

2 Stir the mixture until the paste has fully coated the paper. Keep adding newspaper strips until your mixture is thick and ready to use.

3 Using small lumps of papier mâché, shape your letters from many layers. Press the papier mâché firmly to form the letters, and allow to dry.

4 When the letters are completely dry, they are ready to be decorated. Paint them in bright colours, using poster or acrylic paints. You could also cover them with spots or get creative with lines and swirls.

Drawing Sunflowers

Use the template on p.74 to create a magnificent sunflower picture!

Drawing Sunflowers

You will need:
3B pencil
HB pencil
eraser

1 Trace over the sunflower picture outline on p.74.

2 Use a 3B pencil to define the shape of the leaves, creating areas of light and shade with the weight of the strokes. Add the veins by using an eraser, carefully following any folds and curls.

3 Shade the middle of the flowers with the side of a 3B pencil, then make harder strokes with a sharp HB pencil from the centre outwards. Concentrate on adding detail to the petals – too much shading will make them appear dull.

4 Shade the stalks with long, fine, vertical lines to emphasise the direction of growth. Add darker tones to one side with a 3B pencil to create a three-dimensional effect.

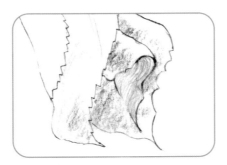

5 Use the side of a 3B pencil to add shading to the water in the vase, then use the eraser to remove the areas where light would bounce off the glass.

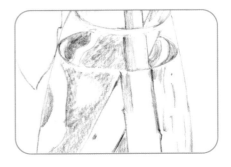

6 Why not use your completed sunflower picture as the centre piece on a greetings card.

73

Decorating Eggs

You will need:
- eggs
- old newspaper
- paintbrush
- acrylic paints
- clean water
- egg cups

1 First, ask an adult to boil your eggs for 15 minutes and then allow the eggs to cool completely.

2 Cover your work area with old newspapers. Use an egg cup to steady your eggs whilst you paint them. To get an even finish, decorate half of your egg and let it dry, before turning it over in the egg cup to paint the other half.

3 Copy the designs shown in this book, or come up with some ideas of your own, using a paintbrush and acrylic paints. Remember to clean your brush with water every time you change colour.

4 The eggs will go bad after a couple of days, so remember to throw them out!

Warning!
Do not eat the eggs. They are for decoration purposes only!

Pompom Bunny

Recreate this funny bunny in five simple steps.

Paper Daffodil

1 Take a sheet of yellow tissue paper and draw around the daffodil petal template (on p.81) six times. Draw around the daffodil leaf template (on p.81) onto green tissue paper four times.
Cut out these parts.

You will need:
green and yellow tissue paper
petal and leaf templates
(see p.81)
green and orange fuzzy sticks
double-sided tape

2 Cut two strips of yellow tissue paper measuring 30 cm (12 in.) long and 6 cm (2½ in.) wide. Roughly fold the tissue paper backwards and forwards to make it look crinkly.

3 Cut an orange fuzzy stick so that it is 10 cm (4 in.) long. Now, bend this over onto itself so that it is 5 cm (2 in.) long.

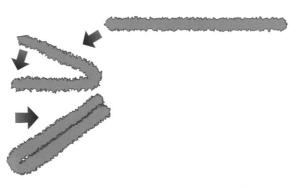

4 Carefully wrap one of the folded lengths of tissue paper around the orange fuzzy stick, taping it in place as you go. Repeat this with the other folded strip, making sure it is slightly lower than the first layer, as shown.

5 Add double-sided tape to the bottom of the six yellow petals. Add these to the base of the second folded cone shape, as shown, spacing them out evenly and making sure they overlap one another slightly.

6 Carefully wind one end of a green fuzzy stick over and around the orange one to join the head of the flower to the stem.

7 Add double-sided tape to the bottom of the four large leaves. Stick these to the green fuzzy stick at the back.

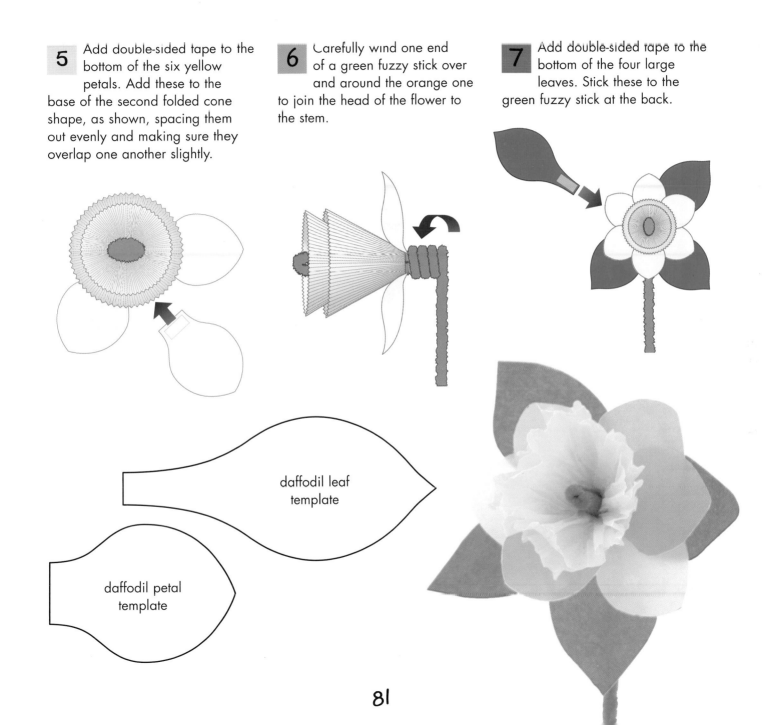

daffodil leaf template

daffodil petal template

5 Use this wing as a template to draw a second wing. Draw around it, and then cut it out.

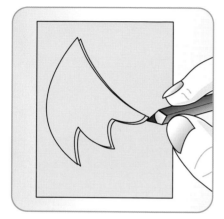

6 On a red piece of felt, draw the chicken's crest and wattle, then carefully cut out these shapes.

7 It is now time to start putting all of the bits together. Stick the two wings onto the spoon just where it starts to join the handle. Make sure you stick on the wings in the right way. Press them down firmly with your fingers.

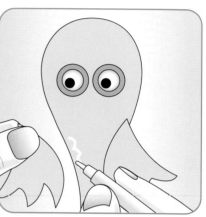

8 Stick the crest to the top of the chicken's head and the wattle level with the tops of the wings (use the picture below as a guide). Then, stick on the beak just below the eyes.

9 Using a black felt pen, draw a line across the chicken's beak. Let the glue dry for a while before playing with him.

Fingerprint Fun!

The sun is shining and all the finger doodle creatures live happily together!

Get Your Hair Cut!

1 Have a boiled egg for breakfast. Be careful how you break open the top. Keep the empty shell.

2 Place the egg into an egg cup to steady it whilst you draw or paint a face on your eggshell. Make the face look as funny as you can.

You will need:
eggshells
egg cups
felt pens, gel pens or acrylic paints
cotton wool
mustard and cress seeds
a water-sprayer

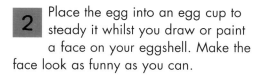

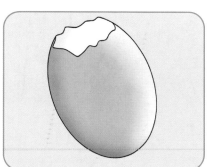

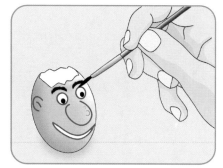

5 Spray some more water on from time to time so the cotton wool doesn't dry out.

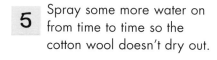

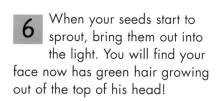

3 Dampen some cotton wool with water and press it gently into the shell.

4 Sprinkle some mustard and cress seeds onto the cotton wool and place it in a warm, dark place like an airing cupboard.

6 When your seeds start to sprout, bring them out into the light. You will find your face now has green hair growing out of the top of his head!

Bunny Puppets

Make a whole family of cute rabbit finger puppets.

7 Glue on the goggle eyes and draw in a little mouth with a black marker pen. Stick the head to the body.

Get Creative!
When you are confident at making Bunny Puppets, why not experiment and make other animals?

8 Turn the rabbit over and glue on a small, fluffy cotton wool tail. Leave the puppet to dry overnight.

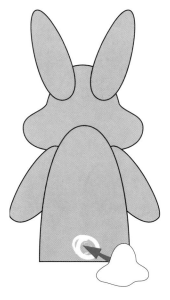

Bunny Puppet templates:

outer ear

inner ear

nose

cheeks

arm

paw

body

chest

head

My Creative Ideas!